WHEN THE SUN ROSE AGAIN

AARAV ANAND

*To the elderly whose voices are often silenced,
whose wisdom is overlooked,
and whose hearts are left to wait.*

*May this book remind you that you are never forgotten,
that your stories matter, and that it is never too late
to find love, belonging, and a new beginning.*

Contents

Foreword

In every corner of the world, there are stories of strength, love, and resilience that often go untold. One such story is that of the elderly, individuals who have lived entire lifetimes, yet find themselves quietly pushed aside as time marches on. It's a harsh reality that many of us don't often see, but it is one that is worth understanding, acknowledging, and changing.

Aarav, at just 13 years old, has crafted a story that speaks to the heart of this issue. Through the eyes of an elderly woman, he brings us face-to-face with the reality of being forgotten by the very people we once nurtured, loved, and cared for. Yet, in the midst of loneliness and abandonment, he shows us that even when the world moves on, there is always room for rediscovery, hope, and renewal.

Aarav's passion for social service and his keen sense of empathy shine through every page, reminding us all that it's never too late to start again, to build new families, and to embrace life, no matter the age.

May this story inspire you to look beyond the surface, to listen to the silenced voices, and to understand that the heart is never too old to love or be loved in return.

Preface

In our **busy, fast-paced world,** it's easy to **overlook the elderly,** the ones who've lived through decades of experiences, yet often find themselves **silenced and forgotten.** As a young writer, I've come to realize how much we have to learn from the stories of our elders, their quiet wisdom, and their unspoken strength.

This book is born from that realization. It began as a story I felt needed to be told, a story of a woman who, after being sent to an old-age home, finds herself starting over in the final chapter of her life. As I wrote her journey, I became deeply moved by her resilience, her courage to embrace a new life, and the friendships she forms in unexpected places.

The inspiration for this story came from my own passion for social service. I wanted to create a story that would not only entertain but also raise awareness about the emotional challenges faced by the elderly, and inspire others to see them in a new light, as individuals with untold stories and unfulfilled dreams.

In writing this book, I hope to remind everyone that it is never too late to start anew, to find a sense of belonging, and to open your heart to life's second chances. I also hope to inspire change, to encourage us all to embrace those around us, regardless of age, and recognize the beauty in every stage of life.

I dedicate this book to the elderly who have been left behind, to those whose stories remain untold, and to the quiet strength they carry within. May this story be a reminder that it's never too late to find love, to find family, and to truly live again.

Acknowledgements

This book would not have been possible without the love, encouragement, and guidance of so many incredible people.

First and foremost, I want to thank my family. Their unwavering support and belief in me have been the foundation of everything I do. To my parents, who taught me the value of empathy, kindness, and understanding, thank you for always encouraging me to follow my heart and to use my voice for good.

To my teachers, who have been a constant source of inspiration and mentorship. Your encouragement in both my writing and my social service journey helped shape this book into something meaningful. You all pushed me to think deeper, to care more, and to believe that I could make a difference.

A special thank you to the elderly individuals whose lives and experiences inspired this story. Though they may never read these words, their silent strength and enduring spirit have touched my heart deeply. This book is a tribute to all of them, and to the countless others who feel forgotten.

I would also like to thank my friends and fellow writers, who have supported me through the highs and lows of the creative process. Your feedback, encouragement, and enthusiasm made every step of this journey more enjoyable.

Finally, I thank all those who read this book and choose to embrace its message, that it is never too late to begin again. May we all be inspired to lift up those around us and recognize the value in every life, no matter the age.

Prologue

When the World Let Go:
What does it mean to grow old?
Is it when your hair turns grey and your steps slow down?
Or is it when the people you love stop seeing you the same way?
She was once the first voice someone looked for in the morning.
She sang lullabies, packed lunchboxes, remembered birthdays, and prayed silently for everyone she loved. Her arms were always open, her lap always warm.
But over time, everything changed.
Like a tree in autumn that slowly loses its leaves, she watched her world become quieter, emptier.
The hands that once reached for her now held someone else.
Her stories were no longer asked for. Her advice no longer needed.
On the day her son got married, she smiled. She wore jasmine in her hair and blessings in her heart.
But deep inside, something felt different.
It was like a soft breeze that told the tree,
"Winter is coming."
They said it kindly, that it was for her comfort, her peace.
An old-age home. A place to rest.
But she wondered,
How can you rest when your heart still remembers the noise of family,
the smell of warm food,
the laughter in shared rooms?
For many days, she sat by the window,
watching the sun rise and set,
just like her hopes.
But then, something beautiful happened.
Like a flower blooming in an unexpected corner,
life began to return.

A kind smile. A shared cup of tea.

A soft voice calling her name again, not because they had to, but because they wanted to.

She realised something.

Life does not end when you grow old.

It simply changes shape.

And even when the world forgets you,

the sky still paints colours,

birds still sing,

and hearts can still find new places to belong.

This is her story.

Not of how she was left behind,

but of how she slowly, gently,

learned to live again.

CHAPTER ONE

THE BITTER AFTER-TASTE

The house was blooming. Quite literally.

Bright strings of marigolds hung from every doorway, the floor shimmered with fresh rangoli designs, and the air smelled of ghee, sandalwood, and jasmine. The kind of smell that made you feel like life was beginning anew. For Savitri, it truly was the happiest day she had seen in years.

Her son, Arjun, was getting married.

"Ma, do you like my sherwani?" Arjun twirled in front of her, grinning like a boy who'd won his first race.

Savitri laughed, adjusting his collar fondly. "You look like your father did on our wedding day, nervous but pretending to be confident."

Arjun chuckled. "Then I'll do my best to live up to it."

Savitri's heart swelled. The warmth of his presence, the sparkle in his eyes, it was everything she had dreamt of. Her son had grown into a fine man. She had raised him alone after his father passed away, giving up everything just to see this day.

Every step of the wedding planning had brought her joy, from choosing the caterer to picking the mandap decorations to helping Riya, her soon-to-be daughter-in-law, select the perfect red for her bridal saree. Even the sleepless nights had been filled with purpose.

The house bloomed with relatives calling out instructions, children running wild, and distant beats of the band rehearsing outside. The wedding was still hours away, but celebrations had already begun.

Her sisters had flown in from Jaipur, her niece from Bangalore. Everyone kept telling her what a wonderful job she had done. And every time someone praised the arrangements, Savitri blushed like a bride herself.

She moved through the crowd with a quiet joy, offering sweets, blessing the bride's family, ensuring everything was just right. She didn't mind the chaos. This kind of chaos was made of laughter, life, and beginnings.

The Haldi ceremony had been especially memorable. Riya's cousins had pulled Arjun aside and smeared turmeric on his cheeks, and he had retaliated by throwing a fistful right onto his mother's saree.

"Oh no, Ma!" he had cried, seeing the golden smear on her blouse.

Savitri had only laughed, "Now I'm blessed too!"

She had worn a saree of her husband's favorite color, peacock blue with gold zari. Every time someone complimented it, she touched the pallu as if it had brought him closer on this special day.

Later that afternoon, as the rituals began, she took a moment to sit down. Her feet ached, and her back longed for rest, but her eyes sparkled as they followed Arjun.

The groom's procession was grand. Dhols beat loudly. The horse Arjun sat on was decorated in red and gold. The sky glowed a soft orange as evening drew near. Riya's family welcomed them with garlands and gifts. She stood proudly, watching her son step forward into a new chapter.

"Ma, come stand beside us!" someone called.

She stood next to Arjun as the priest instructed the couple to take their places. The rituals began: mantras, fire, flowers, and whispered promises. She watched closely, clutching the small silver box of kumkum she had carried since her own wedding.

It was when the photographers began their work that things started to shift.

"Bride's side first!" one of them shouted.

Riya's family gathered, smiling brightly. Her mother, her father, her younger siblings. All clicked, all cheered.

Then came, "Groom's friends!"

Laughter. Boys Arjun had known since college. They hugged him, joked, posed.

Then: "Siblings!"

Arjun's cousins stood beside him. The flash went off again and again.

Savitri stepped forward slightly, waiting. Any moment now.

But the photographer moved on.

"Immediate family!" someone yelled.

The bride's parents took their place once again. Arjun stood in the middle, arms linked with both. More photos.

No one called her.

She took a step back.

The mandap glowed like a golden sun under the canopy of jasmine flowers. Strings of marigolds hung like curtains from the marble pillars, swaying gently in the December wind. Fairy lights blinked like stars that had come too close. The band had long stopped playing, but the guests hadn't left the dance floor. Champagne flowed into tall glasses. Women in sequins laughed. Children in sherwanis chased each other across the lawn.

In the middle of it all sat Savitri. Her hair, grey and neatly tied in a bun, held a single rose, placed there earlier that day by the bride herself.

"Maaji, blue suits you beautifully," Riya had said with a warm smile, tucking the flower in gently. "Today, you are the queen."

Savitri had smiled, touched by the gesture. She wanted to believe it. But as the evening unfolded, she began to realise that queens rarely sat alone in corners while kingdoms were rebuilt without them.

She clutched her handbag tightly in her lap, watching her son Arjun, now someone else's husband. His sherwani shimmered silver under the lights. He looked handsome. Grown. Like a man she didn't fully recognise anymore.

From a distance, Arjun met her gaze briefly, then turned back to his new bride as the photographer instructed them to lean closer for yet another picture.

Savitri's fingers fidgeted with the edge of her saree.

A waiter passed by with a tray of paneer tikka, but she didn't take any.

Riya's cousin noticed. "Ma'am, why don't you rest inside? It's getting a little cold out here."

Savitri nodded. Her voice had gone somewhere quiet. "Yes, perhaps I will."

Inside, the house was quieter. Empty chairs, discarded shawls. She walked to the far end where her son's childhood room stood. She opened the door.

It smelled faintly of old crayons and dust. His trophies still lined the top shelf. A few books she had kept for memory sat on the desk. She sat down on the bed and looked around.

This room had held her whole world once.

She traced the edge of a comic book Arjun had loved as a boy. She looked at the football medal he had won in class five. She touched the blanket she had stitched during his school years.

Laughter floated in from outside. Fireworks lit the sky.

But inside, the silence grew a little louder.

She went to the kitchen and began arranging steel containers, stacking them with leftovers, wiping counters no one had asked her to wipe. Her hands moved from habit, but her mind drifted.

The next morning, she sat by the window with a cup of chai. No one joined her. The bride's family was already gone. Arjun and Riya were getting ready to leave for a short honeymoon.

"Ma, we'll only be gone for a week," Arjun said, distracted. "Riya's office has called her back early."

"Of course, beta," she said, hiding the flicker of disappointment.

That week passed slowly. The walls of the house seemed to press in tighter. The silence had a sound of its own, the absence of footsteps, the echo of a door closing far away, the hum of an unused refrigerator.

When Arjun returned, he was different. He was polite, kind, but hurried.

"Ma, we've decided to stay at the service apartment near Riya's office. It's easier for both of us till our own flat is ready."

Savitri smiled, unsure. "And this house?"

"We'll rent it maybe. Or sell. You've done too much here already."

"And me?"

Arjun hesitated. "Ma, there's this place. Ashray Nivas. It's lovely. Peaceful. They take care of everything. Food, medicines. I've seen it. Just for a little while. Once the flat is sorted, we'll see."

She said nothing.

He added, "You always said you didn't want to be a burden."

She looked at him. Her son. Her world.

"I didn't say I wanted to be forgotten."

He looked away. "It's just for now, Ma."

She nodded slowly. A silence settled between them, the kind that says more than words ever could.

The next morning, she packed her own suitcase.

No one helped.

As she sat in the car, she glanced once more at the window of her old room. The rose plant she had nurtured was blooming. It swayed gently in the wind. Like it was waving goodbye.

She didn't cry. Not yet.

Somewhere deep inside her, something folded quietly. A chapter ended.

And a new, uncertain one began.

As the car carried her away, Savitri closed her eyes and let her mind drift back through the years. She remembered the day she first met Raghav at the college library, his shy smile across the dusty shelves. How he had borrowed her pen and returned it with a note folded like a paper crane: Would you join me for tea?

Her heart fluttered then just as it did now, though for different reasons. She could almost feel his hand sliding into hers, pulling her into a world made of hopes and shared dreams.

That first shy romance led to a small wedding beneath a neem tree. She saw again the yellow turmeric on her cheeks, the garland of marigolds in Raghav's hands, and the promises whispered beneath a cloudless sky.

They had scraped together every rupee to rent a tiny flat in the city, its balcony overlooking a narrow alley where laundry fluttered like colorful pennants. Savitri had cried tears of joy when they hung a small photo of her parents above the simple dining table.

Night after night, they had lain awake listening to rain tap the tin roof. He would hum a lullaby she had sung to him as a child. She would drift to sleep, feeling safe for the first time in her life.

When Arjun arrived, the world had turned brighter. Savitri still felt the pain of labor, but then she had heard his first cry, strong and clear, and all the aches had melted away.

She and Raghav had spent weeks choosing his name, debating on Arjun for his courage, or Kunal for his lotus-like purity. In the end, they had whispered both names beside his tiny blanket until the newborn cooed at the sound of Arjun, and the name stuck.

The early days had been chaotic. Sleepless nights soothed by mornings of laughter as Arjun discovered his fingers, his toes, and the bright world around him. Savitri had embroidered his first blanket with the lotus motif she remembered from her wedding saree. Raghav had teased her that she was creating his future daughter-in-law's trousseau.

They saved for a small house with a courtyard. Savitri had planted jasmine at its edge, saying it would bring sweetness to their home. Under that tree, Arjun had chased butterflies and learned to ride a bicycle. Raghav had taught him to recite poetry at dusk, and Savitri had woven stories of heroes and kindness at bedtime.

Months turned into years. The little flat became a home filled with friends, festivals, and the smell of Savitri's cooking: spicy curries, sweet halwa, crisp cheelas on Sunday mornings. Raghav's laughter echoed through the halls. Arjun grew, tall and curious, always running to his mother with a new fact about the world.

Then one winter morning, Raghav had not woken. A silent heart had stopped in sleep. Savitri had knelt beside him, her tears falling onto his folded hands. Arjun, only five, had asked why Papa was so still.

"That is his way of sleeping forever," Savitri had whispered, holding her son close. "But Papa's love will always be here." She pressed the notes Raghav had written into Arjun's palm, letters to the boy he would never see grow up.

The house felt hollow after that. Savitri had wrapped herself in jasmine-scented memories, teaching her son to be brave, to smile even when the heart felt broken.

She remembered Arjun's first day at school, his trembling hand in hers. She had squeezed it and told him, "You are strong, beta. Even if I'm not always there, know you carry my love with you." He had nodded, tears shining in his young eyes.

And he had grown stronger still. Each report card, each medal, each new friendship was a small triumph. Savitri had lived for those moments, her eyes shining brighter than any diya she lit during festivals.

Back in the present, the car wound through unfamiliar streets. Savitri's heart ached for all those years, years of love, loss, and unspoken joy. She opened her eyes and looked once more at the rose plant in her old room's window, imagining Raghav's gentle voice: "Your garden still blooms, Savitri. And so do you."

She kissed the photo of her husband tucked inside her sweater, whispering, "I'm trying, Raghav." The words carried on the wind as the car doors clicked shut.

The new chapter awaited, its pages blank and uncertain, but Savitri's spirit, forged by decades of laughter and tears, would write every line.

As she stepped onto the grounds of Ashray Nivas the next morning, the memories settled in her chest like a warm ember. The sacred fire of her past guided her forward into the sunrise of her second life.

THE SIGHING EARTH AND A NEW FRIEND

The gates of Ashray Nivas opened with a metallic groan, like a sigh from the earth itself. A quiet building painted in fading cream and green stood in the middle of a large compound dotted with trees that had lost their bloom. The lawn was dry in patches, the fountain in the middle coughed more than it flowed, and the board that read "Ashray Nivas – A Home for the Elderly" was chipped at the edges.

It didn't look like a home. It looked like an afterthought.

Savitri stepped out of the car, her small suitcase in hand. Her bangles jingled faintly, a gentle, familiar music from a different life. The air was thick with the scent of dust and disinfectant. No one came to greet her at the gate. A middle-aged man in a blue uniform stood at a distance, pretending to sweep the pathway but not really trying.

Arjun didn't come in.

"They'll take care of everything, Ma. You'll see. It's just a matter of time," he had said, gripping the steering wheel too tightly, eyes looking everywhere except her face. He'd leaned over to close the car door from the inside. No goodbye hug. No parting words. The engine had started before the door even shut.

And then he was gone.

She stood at the entrance for a long moment, uncertain. The building seemed to watch her silently, unmoved by her presence.

Taking a deep breath, she began to walk.

The reception area was dimly lit, barely animated by the creaking of a fan above and the flicker of a tube light near the stairs. A thin lady in a mustard sari looked up from behind a counter that held a dusty idol of Ganesha and a cracked pen holder.

"New admission?"

Savitri nodded.

"Name?"

"Savitri Mehra."

The woman scribbled something in a large register and handed her a plastic badge with her name on it in smudged ink.

"Room 6. Second floor. Lift doesn't work. You'll have to take the stairs."

Savitri smiled politely. "That's alright."

She took the badge and clipped it to her saree. Her footsteps echoed as she dragged her modest suitcase up the cracked stairway.

The hallway smelled faintly of turmeric, old wood, and some kind of cheap antiseptic. Doors stood half open, revealing glimpses of wheelchairs, shriveled plants on windowsills, and television sets blaring daily soaps at a volume too loud for comfort. Somewhere, someone was coughing endlessly, a rasping, persistent sound. Another room played an old Hindi song, slightly out of tune and haunting.

When she finally reached Room 6, she paused at the door. The number plate was rusted. A single bed, a small cupboard, a plastic chair, and a window looking out to a large banyan tree greeted her.

She set her suitcase down and sat at the edge of the bed. The mattress was stiff. The air was still. The silence was a stranger.

She opened the window. A faint breeze slipped in and touched her cheek. She closed her eyes.

"Raghav," she whispered to the wind, "do you see where your Savitri has come? This isn't the house we dreamt of. There's no tulsi plant in the courtyard, no morning bhajans, no Arjun running around in muddy shoes. Just silence. Just me."

She imagined him standing at the doorway, tall and gentle, arms folded, watching her with those knowing eyes. But when she opened her own, there was only the empty corridor beyond.

The first night was the hardest.

Dinner was served at six. A watery daal, two dry chapatis, and a scoop of overcooked sabzi. The dining hall was filled with the clink of steel plates, low murmurs, and the occasional burst of coughing. No one spoke to her. She sat alone at a corner table, observing the others.

An old man in a checkered sweater kept mumbling to himself. A lady with shaking hands spilled water twice before giving up. A couple sat silently across from one another, not exchanging a word, just staring at their plates like they held answers from the past.

When she returned to her room, she found a note pinned to her door:

Yoga at 7 AM. Common room.

She smiled faintly and pinned it to the wall.

At least there was routine.

But routine was not warmth.

The days blurred into one another. Morning yoga with a stern instructor who barely smiled. Tea at 8:30. Lunch at 12. Evening prayer at 5. Dinner at 6. Lights off by 9.

The staff were trained, but distant. They served, cleaned, and managed, but rarely made eye contact. They were shadows in uniform.

She tried speaking to the other residents. Some nodded and smiled, most returned quickly to their own quiet worlds. Some stared blankly through her, others seemed wrapped in memories that went too deep to explain.

Once, she overheard a lady whispering into a mirror, calling it by the name of her long-lost sister.

This wasn't a home. It was a waiting room for those who had been forgotten.

One afternoon, she sat beneath the banyan tree with her knitting. The thread slipped softly through her fingers, the sound of needles offering some comfort.

"Nice pattern," a voice said.

She looked up. A man in his seventies with a thick moustache, lively eyes, and a playful half-smile stood nearby.

"Name's Dev. You're the new one?"

"Yes," she said, hesitant. "Savitri."

"Don't let the silence get to you," he said, sitting down beside her. "This place grows on you. Like moss."

She laughed. A real one.

Dev raised an eyebrow. "That's better. Most people don't laugh here until week three."

He had been a school principal once. Lost his wife five years ago. Two sons, one in California, one who lived in Delhi but never called.

In Dev, she found her first friend.

He showed her the forgotten corners of Ashray Nivas: a tiny library behind the laundry room with dust-covered books; a rose garden that only bloomed in March; a rusty radio in the common room that played Lata Mangeshkar every Thursday at noon.

They started having tea together every evening. Dev would bring two cups from the canteen, grumbling about how weak it was, and they would sit on the bench under the banyan, watching squirrels chase each other on the branches.

She started writing letters to Raghav. Not to post. Just to feel.

"Dear Raghav,

Today I made tea for someone else. I remembered how you liked yours with two spoons of sugar, even when the doctor said one. Do you remember that summer we got caught in the rain near the gurdwara? I laughed so much that day. Here, it hasn't rained in weeks. But inside me, memories fall like quiet rain.

I don't know when hope will be on my side again.

Yours,

Savitri"

She began to belong.

Not because Ashray Nivas changed, but because she did.

She began to notice little things: the robin's song at sunrise, the crinkle of newspapers in the common room, the soft moan of the lift that never worked.

She offered to help with morning bhajans. She joined the others for carrom even though she never quite got the rules. She began placing fresh flowers near the small temple inside the compound every Friday.

But at night, when she lay on her bed, her hand still reached for the empty space beside her.

"Raghav," she whispered into the stillness, "I'm still learning how to live again. Are you proud of me?"

The banyan leaves rustled gently in answer.

And for now, that was enough.

CHAPTER THREE

A Sudden Storm

Ashray Nivas stood on the edge of the city like a forgotten bookmark in an old, dusty novel. From the outside, it looked serene, rows of neat brick cottages, shaded verandas, and flowering trees that bowed gently in the afternoon breeze. But to Savitri, it still felt like a place where time had stopped... and taken memories hostage.

Her first week passed in quiet observation. The other residents were friendly enough, some cheerful, others locked in their own silences. There was Mrs. Thomas, who sang old English lullabies in the garden; Mr. Kamat, who read the newspaper aloud to himself every morning; and Meera Didi, a former Kathak dancer who now walked with a cane and a storm in her eyes.

But Savitri stayed mostly alone. Her cottage was small, just a small room, a kitchenette, and a little porch where two chairs faced the garden. She'd placed a photo of Raghav on the windowsill and spoke to it every night.

"Raghav, I don't know what I'm doing here," she whispered one evening, the silence thick around her. "Did you ever imagine this would be how I'd grow old? Alone, in a place where every clock ticks too loudly."

That evening, restless and unable to sleep, she wandered down the corridor of the main building. Her slippers padded softly across the stone floor. The walls held framed photographs of Ashray Nivas from decades ago, its first residents, its founders, old festivals celebrated with music and laughter.

One photograph made her stop.

In it, a group of young volunteers stood smiling around a table of books and sweets. In the back row, beside a tall man in a Nehru jacket, stood a man she could never forget.

It was Raghav.

Her breath caught.

She moved closer. The photo was dated 1983. The caption below read, "Founding Day – With the first community volunteers."

Her fingers trembled as they brushed the glass. Raghav had never mentioned this. Never.

Why was he here?

That night, she barely slept. Questions churned in her mind like leaves in a storm. Had Raghav once worked here? Was it a coincidence? Or had he hidden something, a past she had never known?

The next morning, she asked the staff, but no one seemed to know much. Ashray Nivas had changed management several times. Records were incomplete. The photo, they said, had been there for years.

Savitri returned to the hallway again that evening and stood before the frame. She stared at her husband's face, the familiar smile that had once felt like home.

"Why didn't you tell me, Raghav?" she asked softly. "Why were you here? Who were you, before us?"

The questions stayed with her.

In the days that followed, she began exploring Ashray Nivas, not just its gardens and rooms, but its hidden stories. She visited the old storage shed behind the library, where unused furniture and files were kept. The shelves were dusty, filled with yellowed papers and moth-eaten folders.

There, in a metal drawer, she found a file marked *Volunteer Logs – 1980s.*

Her hands shook as she opened it.

There he was. Raghav Mehra. Volunteer ID: 029.

His file included a few faded forms and notes. In one corner, scribbled in pencil, were words that made her heart pound:

"Initiated storytelling sessions for abandoned elders. **Gifted cassette player for Room 7.** Deep personal connection with Mr. S.K. Menon, possible family history? Requested privacy. Withdrawn from service in 1984."

Room 7.

That was the room next to hers.

Later that evening, Savitri sat in the common garden, her thoughts spinning like a thread pulled too tight. She stared at Room 7. Its windows were always shut. Its door always locked.

That night, she stood at its doorstep, holding a copy of the photo she had taken with her phone.

She looked at Raghav's face again.

"Did you leave something behind for me?" she whispered. "Or... did you leave someone behind?"

The wind rustled through the leaves above, and for a moment, it felt like the trees were listening.

She turned the knob.

It was open.

CHAPTER FOUR

ROOM 7

The door creaked as Savitri pushed it open.

Room 7 was steeped in shadows. The curtains were drawn, the air heavy with stillness, as if the room had been waiting, untouched, for years. A soft beam of moonlight slipped through a crack in the window and fell upon a dusty rocking chair.

Savitri stepped in slowly, her sandals brushing over the tiled floor. She didn't know what she was expecting. A letter? A box? A voice from the past?

Instead, there was silence.

She ran her hand across the shelf near the door. Dust clung to her fingers. A stack of old books lay toppled over. Beside it, a rusted cassette player sat still, the plastic yellowed with time.

Her heart skipped a beat.

She remembered the note in Raghav's file: *"Gifted cassette player for Room 7."*

She reached out, half-afraid, and pressed the play button.

For a moment, nothing happened.

Then... a click, a whirr... and a voice.

Crackled. Soft. Gentle.

"If you are listening... perhaps you are someone who feels abandoned. But don't worry, I'm there for you. My name is Raghav Mehra."

Savitri gasped and clutched the edge of the chair. The voice was unmistakable, worn but familiar. It was Raghav. Her Raghav.

"If you are reading this, it means I am no longer here to speak to you in person, and perhaps that is how life works, one chapter ends, and another begins, whether we are ready for it or not. But I ask that you listen closely, for my words are not just a message, but a hope. Maybe you came here, like I did, not by choice but by the cruel hands of life. Maybe, just like me, you have felt the sting of being forgotten, abandoned, or left behind.

I know what you are feeling, those silent, painful nights where the world outside seems to have moved on, and all you are left with is this space, this room, and the echoes of the past. I know what it's like to feel as if the sun has set on your life, and there will never be a dawn again.

But please, hear me when I say: this place is not what it seems.

Ashray Nivas is not a final destination for the forgotten. It is not a tomb for lost souls. It is a garden, waiting to bloom once more.

Let me tell you about my story, the one that led me here. My mother was sent to an old age home many years ago. I was young and naïve, and at the time, I thought I was doing the right thing. My father had passed, and I was struggling to make ends meet. I thought it was the best I could offer her, clean sheets, hot meals, and the comfort of routine. But I was wrong.

The night my mother died, I sat alone in a dark room, overwhelmed by regret. That night, I realized the truth: I had stolen something from her. Not in any grand or cruel way, but by thinking that care was enough. I had stolen her right to be remembered, her right to live with dignity, to be seen not just as someone in need, but as a person with a past, with dreams, with desires. I had abandoned her in a place where she had no voice, no purpose.

And when I realized that, I was struck by an overwhelming sense of guilt. I had failed her in the one way that mattered most, by forgetting that love was not just about providing care, but about honoring her humanity.

Years later, I found myself at Ashray Nivas, not as a visitor or a family member, but as a witness to the lives here. I came with the desire to atone, to make amends for what I had done. I volunteered at first, then stayed. I wrote letters, taught when I could, and planted roses in the garden, my own way of trying to bring life back to this place.

But most of all, I stayed because I knew that this place could become something more. It could become a home. Not just a building with walls, but a sanctuary for souls. And so, I worked, not for recognition, but because I believed, with all my heart, that there was hope in this space. I hoped that one day, someone would walk through these gates with the same longing that I once had, the longing to create, to belong, and to be part of something greater.

And maybe, just maybe, that person is you.

If you are listening to this, know that you were never meant to be forgotten. You were never meant to be pushed aside, to be seen as a burden. You, too, have a place here, a place where you can start again. Where the past does not define you, but the future still holds promise.

Ashray Nivas is not a resting place for the unwanted. It is a garden waiting for someone to plant the seeds of love again. You are not here by mistake. You are here because there is work to be done. And that work, that purpose, is to build something beautiful together.

When I first arrived here, I saw only the cracks and the peeling paint. But over time, I came to understand that the cracks are not imperfections, they are the places where light can enter. And light, my dear, is what we need most. The light of understanding, of kindness, of shared stories and moments. The light of knowing that we are not alone, that we never were.

I wish I could be there to see you, to help you take the first steps. But if you are hearing this, know that I am with you in spirit. You are not abandoned. You are not forgotten. You are meant to begin again.

I have left this message as a reminder, a seed planted in the soil of this home, hoping that it will grow into something wonderful. Please do not let the darkness of this place overshadow the light that is waiting to shine. The sun will rise again, just as it did for me, and

just as it will for you.
And when the sun rises again, let us be ready to bloom.
Ashray Nivas is not a resting place for the unwanted.
It is a garden waiting for someone to plant seeds of love again.
With all my love and hope,
Raghav Mehra"

Savitri's eyes blurred with tears.

The cassette ended abruptly with a dull click.

Savitri sat frozen.

This wasn't just a visit. Raghav had belonged here. He had come to heal something that had haunted him, something he had never shared, not even with her. A piece of his soul had been tied to this place long before she ever stepped through its gates.

That night, Savitri didn't sleep.

She sat by her window, staring at the same moon that had once watched over Raghav. Her fingers trembled as she held the old photograph. So many years together, and yet so much she didn't know.

But somehow, the discovery didn't feel like betrayal.

It felt like a bridge.

A thread connecting her to this strange new home. If Raghav had found meaning here, maybe... just maybe, she could too. Maybe... the Sun Rose Again?

THE FIRST SEED

The next morning, the rays of the sun streamed through the half-opened window blinds, casting golden stripes across Savitri's wrinkled face. She had barely slept. Raghav's frame lay beside her pillow. The final lines of what Raghav had said, rang again and again in her heart:

"Ashray Nivas is not a resting place for the unwanted.
It is a garden waiting for someone to plant seeds of love again."

She looked around her room, not a cell anymore, but a starting point. Her fingers brushed the table's edge as she stood slowly, pulled her cardigan around her shoulders, and walked outside.

The corridors smelled of stale disinfectant and boiled lentils. But today, she didn't walk with her eyes cast down. She observed. A nurse passed by humming to herself. An old man in a wheelchair watched the ceiling fan with vacant eyes. A woman sat by the staircase, muttering to herself. The place felt... tired. But underneath the silence, she could sense something waiting. Raghav's words had lit a small fire inside her.

In the common lounge, a soft-spoken volunteer named Sameer was helping Mrs. Lobo with a jigsaw puzzle. Savitri watched from afar. A tall bookshelf in the corner held books too dusty to be loved, and a faded piano stood silently, like a forgotten ghost of laughter.

"Mrs. Savitri?" Sameer looked up and smiled. "Would you like to join?"

Savitri hesitated, then walked over. "Not for the puzzle," she said. "But may I talk to you later?"

"Of course," he nodded, surprised.

That afternoon, Savitri sat in the garden. The roses Raghav had planted were wilting, petals yellowed and curled. She gently touched one bloom, remembering his words about planting seeds of love. Was this where he had sat, years ago? Was this the same bench?

Suddenly, a familiar voice interrupted her thoughts.

"Boring place, isn't it?"

She turned. A sharp-eyed woman with frizzy white hair and a bright orange scarf stood behind her. "I'm Anjali. New-ish. You?"

"Savitri," she said, smiling softly. "Yes... new-ish too."

"I saw you at breakfast. You looked like you were solving all the world's problems inside your head."

Savitri laughed quietly. "Maybe just this place's problems."

Anjali raised an eyebrow. "You think this place has hope?"

"I don't know. But I think my husband thought so."

The two women talked until the sun dipped low and the garden lights flickered on. Savitri found herself sharing Raghav's letter. Anjali listened, then placed a hand over hers.

"If you're starting something here, I want in."

Later that evening, Savitri walked into the dining hall. She approached Mrs. Gupta, the stern woman who always sat alone counting her pills.

"Would you like to come to the garden tomorrow?" she asked.

"Why?" Mrs. Gupta snapped.

"I want to begin something new. You once used to teach Bharatanatyam, didn't you? Perhaps you could show us a few hand gestures?"

Mrs. Gupta blinked. Then her shoulders softened. "I haven't danced in thirty years."

"Then maybe it's time," Savitri whispered.

One by one, she approached others.

Razia Begum, who once ran a spice shop in Hyderabad, offered to teach everyone how to make garam masala.

Even the silent Mr. D'Souza nodded when Savitri asked if he could help fix the garden bench.

That night, alone in her room, Savitri remembered what Raghav had said:

"You were never meant to be forgotten.
You were meant to begin again."

She sat down at her desk. On a fresh sheet of paper, she wrote:

*"When the Sun Rose Again – Chapter One.
Today, I remembered how it feels to begin."*

As she signed her name at the bottom, the first tears fell, not of pain, but of gratitude. Outside, the roses quivered slightly in the breeze. The moon peeked over the trees, and Ashray Nivas, for the first time in a long time, felt alive.

CHAPTER SIX

WHEN THE SUN ROSE AGAIN

Morning at Ashray Nivas had transformed. It no longer carried the stillness of forgotten time, but a gentle hum of life, tea cups clinking, footsteps pacing in the garden, and the soft sound of laughter weaving through the air. The silence that once lingered like a heavy blanket had been replaced by voices filled with warmth and welcome. "Good morning!" echoed through the halls, and "Did you sleep well?" was met with a genuine smile, not just polite formalities.

It all began in the quietest way, as all the best things do.

Ammaji was the first to respond. The eldest resident of Ashray Nivas, she had always been a quiet figure, her prayers whispered softly under the shade of the neem tree. But one morning, Savitri walked up to her with a box of delicate bangles.

"These were my mother's," Savitri said. "I thought you might like one."

Ammaji's eyes flickered, a sharp contrast to her usual silence. "Why?"

"Because your hands remind me of hers," Savitri answered, her smile warm and understanding. "Strong, yet still so graceful."

There was a pause, and then, as though moved by an unseen force, Ammaji held out her wrist.

From that day forward, Ammaji began joining the morning walks, her once-muted presence brightened by colorful shawls and eyes softened by time. Though she still didn't speak much, she was no longer alone in the shadows.

Then came Dinesh Uncle, who had once been a celebrated classical singer. He claimed his voice had grown too tired and that no one wanted to hear the old songs anymore. But Savitri saw something others didn't. She asked him to teach her a tune each evening, and soon, one by one, the others began to join. What started as a hesitant hum under the stars grew into a joyous music circle.

On Thursdays, under the banyan tree, they sang together, old film songs, bhajans, lullabies. Even those who didn't sing came just to listen, their hearts swaying to the rhythm of nostalgia. Some cried, some closed their eyes, letting the melodies fill the spaces where memories had once faded. In that moment, music became their shared language.

Savitri, always brimming with new ideas, had also asked Mr. Mehra, the warden, if she could paint a mural in the hallway. He had raised an eyebrow but, seeing her resolve, gave her his approval.

One evening, Savitri invited all the members of Ashray Nivas to spend the evening together.

The evening at Ashray Nivas was unlike any other. The air, cool and gentle, carried a sense of anticipation that hummed through the courtyard. The residents, once quiet and isolated in their routines, were now gathering with an energy that had been dormant for far too long. There was something special about tonight, something that felt like the turning of a new page.

Savitri stood at the center, watching as the courtyard slowly filled with life. The once-silent corners of Ashray Nivas were now filled with soft laughter and murmurs of excitement. A festive spirit had taken over, and even the usually reserved nurses were setting down their duties to join the gathering.

"Tonight," Savitri called out, her voice soft but commanding, "we share stories, songs, and memories. Tonight, we celebrate life...together."

A cheer rippled through the group, and slowly, they gathered in a loose circle, with the warm glow of lanterns casting shadows across their faces. At the front of the circle, Radha, the retired actress with a flair for drama, smiled mischievously.

"You know, Savitri, you always know how to bring everyone together," she said, her voice rich with affection. "And we all know I'm the best storyteller around. Shall I start?"

Laughter filled the air as Radha began her tale of an unforgettable mishap during one of her first stage performances. She spun a story of how she had tripped over a stage prop, causing a scene that had the entire audience laughing instead of clapping. She mimicked her younger self's dramatic flair, causing everyone to burst into uncontrollable laughter.

As the laughter settled, Dinesh Uncle, the former classical singer, stood up with a grin. "Ah, it seems like we have an actress in our midst," he said, his voice booming. "But what about a song? A little music to keep the energy flowing?"

Savitri's eyes twinkled. "Dinesh Uncle, I think it's time for you to shine."

With a deep breath, Dinesh Uncle started singing a soulful bhajan. His voice, though weathered by time, still held the rich, melodic quality of his youth. It filled the courtyard, weaving through the trees, as others joined in, humming along or swaying gently to the rhythm. The song was simple, yet its warmth enveloped everyone, reminding them of their roots.

Radha, ever the enthusiast, clapped her hands. "Now, that's the spirit! But I think it's time we turn up the tempo a bit, don't you think?"

And just like that, the pace shifted. With the beat of the dholak provided by one of the volunteers, the energy in the courtyard surged. The residents began to rise from their seats, slowly at first, testing the rhythm, and then with more confidence. Veerji, the retired teacher, stood up and extended his hand to Savitri. "Shall we, Savitri?" he asked, a playful glint in his eye.

With a grin, Savitri took his hand, and they joined the others in the growing circle. The rhythm quickened, and suddenly, Ammaji, who had remained quiet and seated under the neem tree, surprised everyone. She stood, her old feet shuffling slightly as she joined the group. Her hands, once stiff with age, moved gently to the beat of the music.

"Ammaji!" Savitri called out, her voice filled with joy. "You're dancing!"

Ammaji gave a small, shy smile, her frail arms lifting in time with the music. "I never thought I would," she murmured, her voice softer than the rest. "But something feels different tonight."

The others cheered her on, and soon, Ammaji's slow movements became more fluid. Her hands, draped in the bangles Savitri had given her, shimmered in the light. The softness in her movements was almost like poetry, graceful yet filled with strength, a silent testament to her years of endurance.

"Look at her," Radha whispered to Savitri. "She's glowing."

Savitri smiled, watching Ammaji with admiration. "She's always had the power to shine. Sometimes, we just need the right moment to let it out."

The courtyard was now alive with dancing. Some moved with grace, others with more hesitation, but everyone was together in the shared joy of the moment. Ammaji, who had once sat silently under the tree, now danced among them, her once solitary presence woven into the vibrant fabric of the community.

The words hung in the air, soft and intimate. The group fell silent, absorbing the beauty of the verses. Even the nurses, who were usually so focused on their duties, stood still, their eyes filled with emotion.

Savitri looked around at the faces illuminated by the lanterns, the laughter lines, the eyes filled with memories, the hands clasped together in unity. She could feel the depth of connection in that silence, a bond that had grown stronger with each shared moment.

Then, to her surprise, Ammaji spoke again, her voice a whisper but clear.

"I remember... once, my husband and I used to dance like this, under the stars. It was a long time ago, but tonight, it feels like he's here with me."

The group was silent, all eyes on Ammaji. Her words were a quiet confession, a shared memory that tied them all together in a way words couldn't express. It wasn't just the stories or the dancing that had brought them together, it was the shared experiences of love, loss, and hope.

Savitri approached her, placing a gentle hand on Ammaji's shoulder. "You're never alone here, Ammaji. We're all family now."

And as the night wore on, the dancing, the stories, and the laughter didn't stop. The courtyard of Ashray Nivas had become a place of joy, a place where the residents had learned to live again, not through their pasts but through the shared moments that connected them all. Each of them, from Dinesh Uncle to Ammaji, had found a piece of themselves in the company of others.

As the evening came to a close, Savitri stood at the edge of the garden, watching the residents head back to their rooms. The wind rustled the leaves, carrying with it the echoes of the night, a night of dancing, storytelling, poetry, and connection.

Savitri whispered to the night, her heart full, "This place... it was always meant to bloom."

And as if in reply, the breeze carried her words, rustling the trees, wrapping the courtyard of Ashray Nivas in a peaceful, contented embrace.

And then Savitri saw the Sun melting to the peaks of the mountains as they danced, knowing that the Sun will come for them again...knowing that the Sun will Rise Again.

CHAPTER SEVEN

SEASONS GO BY, SO DID TIME

The seasons no longer rushed past Savitri, they strolled gently now, like old friends who had learned to appreciate quiet pauses.

Ashray Nivas, too, had changed with time. It was no longer the same home she had walked into years ago, carrying grief like an invisible suitcase. No, this place had bloomed, and so had she. The once-fading corridors were now lined with laughter, color, music, and murals that told stories far louder than the silence that once ruled.

Savitri had grown older. Her bones ached more. Her walks took longer. But her smile, that warm stretch of calm across her face, had only deepened. She still wore crisp cotton sarees and tucked a jasmine flower behind her ear. Her voice had grown softer, but when she spoke, people listened, as if her words came sprinkled with the wisdom of every sunrise she had seen from the window of Room 6.

Every January, like clockwork, a large brown envelope would arrive with Arjun's neat handwriting in the corner.

The photo inside was always of her grandson.

This year, he stood beside a bicycle with a missing front tooth and a cheeky grin. His name was Anay, and though Savitri had never held him in her arms, she had memorized every change in his face year after year, the way his hair grew curlier, how his legs looked longer, and how his smile began to resemble Arjun's.

The note that came with the photo was brief.

"Ma, we moved into a new house last month, near the school. Riya's keeping busy with work. Anay won a small painting competition! Hope you're well. Love, Arjun."

No invitation followed.

No mention of, "Why don't you come stay with us now?"

But Savitri had long stopped expecting that.

She'd learned to fold each year's photograph carefully, slide it into the little wooden box under her bed, alongside Raghav's unsent letters, old bangles, and one single sock knitted by a resident long gone.

It wasn't bitterness she felt anymore. It was just acceptance.

And truth be told, Ashray Nivas had become more of a family than her own blood ever had.

The mornings still began with the clink of teacups and soft footsteps in the courtyard. Ammaji, now wrapped in thicker shawls and a permanent scowl softened by age, still claimed the bench under the neem tree. She'd scold anyone who stepped on the grass barefoot, unless it was Savitri. For her, Ammaji always had a second cup of ginger tea ready.

Radha had started a book club, though half the time they discussed the endings before anyone finished reading.

Dinesh Uncle, whose fingers now trembled, no longer played the harmonium, but he still sang. Sometimes off-key, sometimes whispering, but always with a heart that made people close their eyes and listen.

A new resident, Mr. Yadav, had once worked as a stage actor in Lucknow. He now performed mini-monologues in the evenings near the banyan tree, making everyone laugh with his dramatic flourishes. He had taken a fond liking to Savitri, often calling her "Madam Director" for the way she'd raise her eyebrows when he overacted.

On most evenings, the courtyard would fill with warmth and candlelight. Plastic chairs would be dragged out, old shawls wrapped around shoulders, and someone would eventually say, "Let's tell stories tonight."

And they would.

About a train journey taken forty years ago. About the day a soldier returned home. About stolen mangoes from a childhood orchard. About heartbreaks that never got spoken of until now.

One such evening stood out, etched in Savitri's memory like a pressed flower in a book.

CHAPTER EIGHT

THE NIGHT OF LANTERNS

It was Diwali, but the air at Ashray Nivas felt different that year. Peaceful. Sacred.

Instead of fireworks, they lit paper lanterns, each resident decorated their own. The sky soon filled with floating lights, like tiny souls ascending with wishes and memories.

Once the lanterns were gone, they sat in a circle in the courtyard. No one said anything for a while. Just listened to the wind rustling through the trees.

Then Savitri spoke.

"My grandson won a painting competition," she said quietly, "and I've never heard his voice."

No one interrupted.

She smiled. "But I have heard Ammaji's lullabies. I've seen Radha cry at the last page of a book. I've watched Dinesh Uncle sing until even the stars felt closer."

Ammaji reached out and took Savitri's hand in hers.

Dinesh cleared his throat. "Time for some shayari, no?"

He recited a poem about aging, a funny, bittersweet rhyme that ended with:

"Hair turned white, or perhaps it's time to cleanse the heart,
In old age, friendship is the most precious treasure of all."

They laughed. They clapped. Radha wiped a tear.

Mr. Yadav performed a short scene from a play about a grandfather and his stubborn cow.

And then, slowly, music began to play from a speaker.

Old Hindi songs.

They didn't dance fast, but they danced.

Ammaji swayed on her chair.

Savitri raised her arms and moved her fingers gently to the tune.

Mr. Mehra, the once-strict warden, joined in too, barely keeping up but smiling like he hadn't in years.

There was no audience, no stage. But it was a performance of hearts.

Later that night, when most had gone to bed, Savitri sat alone on the swing under the banyan tree.

She looked up at the sky and whispered, "I'm still here, Raghav."

And though the wind didn't carry a reply, it circled gently around her, like an old friend resting its head on her shoulder.

Life wasn't perfect.

Her knees hurt in the mornings. Her heart sometimes longed for things she could not reach. But she had built something here, something that made her life full.

She didn't know how many more years she had left. But she knew this:

She would spend them at Ashray Nivas.

With people who shared memories instead of regrets.

With voices that sang her back to life.

With the rising sun, and the quiet swing, and the brown envelope that came once a year.

Home wasn't always made of blood.

Sometimes, it was made of belonging.

And Savitri belonged.

CHAPTER NINE

"WHAT DO YOU DO THERE ALL DAY?"

It began with a question.

"Dadi, what do you do all day there?"

That was what Anay asked during one of Arjun's rare video calls. He was now nine, all elbows and questions, with an impatient curiosity that made Savitri laugh.

"I live" she had said, smiling.

But that question lingered in her mind like a bookmark.

What did she do all day?

She sat with Ammaji beneath the neem tree, helped Radha pick poetry books from the shelf, watched Dinesh Uncle drift into melodies, listened to Mr. Yadav rehearse soliloquies, and sipped ginger tea while the birds rehearsed their own morning chorus.

She remembered laughter echoing off the painted walls. She remembered the day they tied balloons to walkers and wheelchairs for Holi. She remembered "Sunrise Notes" tucked beneath pillows, the night lanterns that rose like blessings, and the story circles where silence became story.

It wasn't just living, it was life itself, in all its layers.

And so, one cold December morning, Savitri took out the old cloth-bound diary from her drawer, sharpened a pencil, and wrote on the rusty pages:

"Ashray Nivas: Where the Sun Rose Again. Chapter 9"

She wrote at the window in the early mornings, when the fog still touched the garden and the rest of the world hadn't yet stirred.

She wrote about how she arrived, with silence packed between her bones.

She wrote about Raghav, and his letter that changed everything.

About Ammaji's bangles, and Dinesh Uncle's first hesitant note.

About Radha and the library.

About the Spring Mela, the badly sung birthday song, the mural that bloomed with names like leaves across time.

Each chapter was not just a story, it was a soul. A person.

Some still lived at Ashray Nivas.

Some had moved on, either to other cities, or other worlds.

But Savitri wrote them all in.

Even their absences became part of the pages.

She interviewed residents in the garden. She scribbled notes while waiting for her tea to cool. She borrowed a typewriter from a volunteer who visited on weekends and slowly typed out every page.

Click. Clack. Pause. Click.

It became the music of her days.

A Book of Belonging

At first, she meant it to be just for herself, a gift to her own heart, so that it would not forget.

But one evening, Mr. Mehra, the warden, noticed the growing pile of typed pages on her table.

"You've been writing a lot, Mrs. Savitri," he said.

She nodded, slightly bashful. "Just something small."

He flipped through a few sheets. Then more. Then sat down with a cup of tea and read until the sun disappeared.

When he looked up, his eyes shimmered.

"This is not small," he said quietly. "This is... us."

Soon, Savitri was left with the last chapter of her book which she named "When the Sun Set Softly".

CHAPTER TEN

A Love Letter to Life, to Loss, to Belonging : A Soliloquy in Ink

Time had passed like a slow-moving river, carving the walls of Ashray Nivas gently, not with violence but with quiet devotion.

Savitri had grown older, her hair now entirely silver, skin like parchment, hands trembling even as she lifted a teacup. But her eyes, those stayed the same. Alive. Aware. Watching the lives she had helped awaken flourish all around her.

Years had ripened the home into something extraordinary. No longer a place where old people were left behind, it had become something else. A haven. A library of living stories. A blooming sanctuary.

And at the center of it all still sat Savitri, though now mostly in her room, wrapped in shawls and memory.

The winters had returned, gentler than before. But with them came an illness, quiet, persistent. The kind that doesn't shout, just gently warns.

She knew. This would be her last season.

But she was not afraid.

She had one thing left to do.

She began to write the final chapter of her book.

She wrote slowly, one stroke at a time, every word pulled from the deepest corners of her heart.

A love letter to life, to loss, to belonging.

"They said old age was the ending of the story. But no one told me that it could also be the most beautiful chapter.

I arrived at Ashray Nivas a ghost of myself. I was still breathing, still walking, but my soul had curled up like a frightened child in a dark corner.

And yet... even shadows cannot stop sunlight forever. The first flicker came from Raghav's letter. My beloved. You had left this world, but your words waited for me like a lamp left lit in the dark. You said this place was a garden. I thought you were mistaken.

But gardens don't begin in bloom. They begin in silence, in soil, in patience.

It was slow. Ammaji's silence. Dinesh Uncle's forgotten voice. The others whose eyes avoided mine because their hearts carried wounds too deep to speak aloud. We were not people, not yet. We were pieces. But pieces can come together.

I gave Ammaji a bangle and she gave me her quiet loyalty. I asked Dinesh Uncle to sing and the wind hummed with his notes. We painted the halls. We laughed. We mourned. We learned to live again, not the way we had before, but anew. With less pride and more presence. With fewer expectations and more gratitude.

I watched people change here. Radha began writing poetry again. Mehra ji cried openly during bhajans. I even saw Shanti Kaki dance one night under the moonlight, her arthritis forgotten in the rhythm of an old ghazal. And I, wept.

Not from pain. From awe.
You see, people think we become less as we grow old.
But I have learned... we become more.
We carry more stories, more wisdom, more surrender.
We learn to forgive not just others, but ourselves.
Sometimes, I still wish Arjun had taken me back. That
he would have looked past his discomfort and seen his
mother as more than a burden. But he didn't. And now, I
don't blame him.
Because if he had, I would never have known this life.
I would never have met Anay through his photographs. I
would never have understood what it truly means to build
a home, not of bricks, but of souls.
I was not left here. I was planted.
And I bloomed.
This book is my gift. To Ashray Nivas. To those who
feel forgotten. To those who believe their best years are
behind them. I want you to know: you are not the ashes.
You are the spark. You are not the ending. You are the
encore.
Let them call us old. Let them count our wrinkles. Let
them forget our birthdays.
We will still dance.
We will still sing.
We will still fall in love, with mornings, with each
other, with the memory of who we used to be and the
grace of who we've become.
And when we're gone, we'll remain, in recipes
whispered, in songs sung under trees, in the softness we
leave behind.
I don't know if I'll finish this letter. My hands are
tired, and the sun has begun to set outside my window.
But I'm not afraid anymore.
Because I've lived fully. And because love, once
planted, doesn't die. It grows in the spaces we nurtured.

It grows... here."
She turned the page one last time. Wrote:
"To the next person who arrives here, afraid and
alone
Welcome.
You are not at the end.
You are at the beginning."

She paused.

The clock ticked gently. A soft breeze rustled the curtain.

And then she signed it:

"With all the love I have known,
– Savitri Mehra."

She leaned back.

Her hand slid from the paper.

And like someone slipping into a long-awaited sleep, Savitri let go.

Her breath slowed.

A final smile lingered on her lips.

And then, quietly, as the last word on her final page was still drying in ink, she passed...quietly...peacefully...she left everything behind.

A nurse found her at dawn, the window slightly ajar, the scent of marigolds drifting in.

They did not scream or panic.

They sat beside her. Held her hand. Closed her eyes gently, like you would close the final page of a well-loved book.

And beside her diary, on the last page, was written:

"When the Sun Rose Again."

The book was published six months later. It became a national phenomenon.

Translated into 18 languages. Taught in schools. Whispered in hospital corridors and sung by street musicians.

It changed how people saw ageing.

It changed how families saw the elderly.

It changed everything.

Anay, now ten, read it aloud to his classmates. When asked what it meant to him, he said:

"It means the sun doesn't just rise outside. It rises inside us."

"My Dadi taught me that."

CHAPTER ELEVEN

WITH LOVE, PAPA

Dear Anay,

By the time you read this, you will be old enough to understand things that I took far too long to learn. I've always told you stories of achievements, victories, and milestones, but today, I write to you not with pride, but with regret.

It's about your grandmother, my Ma, Savitri.

You've seen her photograph on the mantle. The one with gentle eyes and a soft smile. That smile once held me when I cried, fed me when I forgot the world, and loved me with a patience so vast that I mistook it for permanence. I thought she'd always be there.

But I left her behind.

She lived the last years of her life in a place called Ashray Nivas, an old-age home. Not because she wanted to, but because I didn't make space for her in mine. We moved to a bigger house, had room for more furniture, but somehow not for the woman who built my first home with her hands and hope.

I told myself she'd be happier with her own people, with friends her age. I justified it. I wrapped my guilt in logic.

But guilt has a way of seeping through even the tightest justifications.

Every year, she sent me letters, light, cheerful, sometimes with little poems or notes from her "Sunrise Notes." She never complained. Not once. She only ever asked about you, how you were growing, if your cough had gone, if you were learning to draw.

She asked me to kiss your forehead on her behalf.

I didn't visit her enough.

And the last time I did, she was gone. All that was left was her book, *When the Sun Rose Again*. I couldn't read it for months. I was too ashamed. When I finally did, I wept like a child.

Anay, that book is not just words, it is a heartbeat. Her heartbeat. It's her rising again, not in grandeur, but in grace. It is laughter on tired mornings, music on forgotten afternoons, and hope tucked into drawers like folded letters.

She died writing her last chapter. Not of sadness, but of peace. Of purpose.

And yet, I carry a hollow space inside me, a space shaped like her. I see her in your gentleness, in the way you offer your hand before someone asks for help. I hear her in your laughter, in your silence, in the drawings you stick on the fridge.

I failed her.

But I write this to you so you won't fail those who love you quietly. Don't wait till people are gone to love them out loud. Don't leave gratitude unspoken. Don't trade presence for comfort.

Someday, you'll grow up and build your own life. In that life, make room for those who built you. Let them grow old near you, not away from you. Let your children know their roots, not just their branches.

Ma is gone now, but her love lives on in this letter, in you, in every sun that rises with a second chance.

With love,

Papa

Author's Note

Dear Readers,

When I first sat down to write this book, I only had a vague picture of an old woman standing alone in a corridor of a silent old-age home. I did not yet know her name. I did not yet know her grief. And I certainly didn't know that she would soon become a light for others, and for me.

Savitri's journey began in silence but ended in symphony. In her, I saw strength wrapped in softness, resilience cloaked in sorrow, and love born not of perfection but of persistence. As she walked the halls of Ashray Nivas, planting stories and sunlight into forgotten hearts, she reminded me, and I hope she reminded you, that life doesn't end with age, it simply starts again...

Thank you for walking with her. Thank you for believing in her, even when the world around her did not.

There is something we don't talk about enough.

Not in schools. Not in boardrooms. Not even around dinner tables.

We don't talk about regret, the kind that comes not from things we've done, but from the people we've slowly stopped seeing.

We build lives, raise families, chase dreams, and in the rush of it all, we forget those who once stood quietly behind us, watching, cheering, waiting. The people who whispered encouragements when we stumbled. The ones who held the corners of our childhood with both hands.

We call them "old." We call them "past."
And one day, we stop calling them at all.

This book was born out of that silence.

It began as a whisper, a story of one woman left behind in a home meant for endings. But it became something more. It became a garden. A memory. A reminder.

That every elder has a name. A story. A history not written in ink but in the lines on their face and the scars they carry silently.

Savitri could be anyone's mother. Anyone's grandmother. She was full of pain, yes, but also full of light. She was not perfect, and she didn't need to be. What mattered was that she rose again, not in grandeur, but in grace. And in doing so, she lifted others.

So, if you've ever loved someone and left too long a silence between your words, this book is for you.

If there's someone still waiting, an Ammaji, a Dinesh Uncle, a quiet woman by a window, go to them.

Not because they are nearing their end,
but because you can still be a part of their middle.

Let this story not be one you simply close at the final page. Let it be something you carry, in your phone call today, in your visit tomorrow, in your letter tucked between clothes.

Let it be the push that helps you choose presence over apology.

And if, by the end, this book made you cry, let the next step be something more powerful than tears:

Let it be action.

Because someday, when your own hands tremble and your voice fades, you too will hope that someone remembers you not just for what you once were, but for who you still are.

And maybe then, just then...

When the sun rises again, it will rise with your name on someone's breath.

With all my heart,
Aarav

Sunrise Notes : The Unsent Mails

As Savitri wrote letters and left them around Ashray Nivas, many of them were never shared in the story. Here are a few more "Sunrise Notes":

"*To the girl who never visits her grandfather anymore: He still sets a plate for you every Sunday.*
To the nurse who thinks no one notices her: We see your kindness, even when you rush.
To my son, Arjun: I forgive you. I love you. I wish you'd brought him to see me once, but I understand why you didn't.
To the mirror: Thank you for showing me the lines on my face. They are my medals of love.
To the sky: I waited all my life to see you blush in orange every morning. Why did I never look up before?"

More Excerpts From Savitri's Book

"I used to think old age was the end of everything. But now, I think it is the beginning of the truth."
"I have seen people cry for yesterday. I have learned to dance with today."
"A bed is just a bed until someone tucks in your blanket and says goodnight."
"We are not abandoned. We are paused. And some of the best stories are told in pauses."
"Raghav, you didn't leave me. You led me home."

Reflections From Ashray Nivas

"Ashray Nivas is not a resting place for the unwanted. It is a garden waiting for someone to plant seeds of love again."

Many people ask if Ashray Nivas is real. The answer is: Yes. And no.

It is not a specific building with a postal address. But it is real in every place where the forgotten are remembered again. It is real wherever the old are not discarded but embraced, not silenced but listened to.

Ashray Nivas exists in every smile we give an elder. In every story we choose to listen to, even if we've heard it before. It lives in nursing homes, in family dining tables, and sometimes, in the smallest moments of connection between generations.

If even one reader decides to pick up the phone and call their grandparent after this book, then Ashray Nivas lives again.

Remembering In Poetry

(A Poem Inspired by Savitri's Story)
>   In a home where silence used to stay,
Where dusty halls saw no child play,
An old woman sat with memories worn,
Of lullabies sung and sarees torn.

>   Her name was Savitri, with eyes so deep,
She bore the weight of wounds that weep.
Sent away, not with hate, but fear,
A burden, not a blessing near.

>   Ashray Nivas, a house of rest,
Held stories lost in each chest.
But from her soul, a spark was stirred,
By a letter's love, by a long-lost word.

>   She wore her pain like a gentle shawl,
But kindness bloomed where tears would fall.
A bangle given, a song once sung,
Revived the hearts that once felt wrung.

>   With Ammaji's prayer and Dinesh's song,
The home found rhythm, the days grew long.
Murals painted, a springtime fair,
Laughter and life filled the stale air.

>   She danced not fast, but with steady grace,
In stories told and each embrace.
"Sunrise Notes" beneath the door,
Turned sorrow into something more.

>   Years went by, as they often do,
Leaves turned gold, and friendships grew.
She aged like wine, both wise and warm,
A quiet sun after the storm.

>   Her son sent pictures once a year,
But never showed, never came near.
Still, she smiled, and held no rage,

She wrote her heart on every page.
    Her book grew thick, her hands grew thin,
Yet love still glowed beneath her skin.
And as she penned her final line,
The moon was high, the stars aligned.
    She whispered soft, not with disdain,
"I bloomed, my loves, despite the pain."
And with her last breath, not in vain,
The sun within her rose again.
    So if you find this tale today,
Don't turn in guilt, don't look away.
Hold your elders, hear their cries,
Before they speak through starlit skies.
    Because love, when given, breaks no chain,
And hope begins... when the sun rose again.

The Legacy

This book is more than fiction. It's a mission.

If Savitri's story touched you, consider volunteering at an old-age home, writing to an elder, or simply spending an hour listening. Time is the most generous gift we can offer.

New Beginnings : The Heart Of The Story

At first glance, When the Sun Rose Again may seem like a story about endings. The last chapter of life. The closing of a door. The echo of voices that have grown quiet. And yes, the book lives within the twilight hours of people who have lived, lost, and lingered.

But beneath the soft melancholy of its pages lies something else, something steady, gentle, and quietly powerful: new beginnings.

This story is not about death. It is about rebirth. It is not about loneliness, it is about rediscovery. Savitri, and every character within Ashray Nivas, teaches us that there are parts of our soul still waiting to awaken, no matter how old we are, no matter how broken.

A beginning doesn't always look like a newborn's cry or a wedding bell. Sometimes, it looks like a bangle being gifted under a neem tree. Sometimes, it is a song shared in a cracked voice, or a laugh that escapes after years of silence. Sometimes, it is just someone remembering your name.

Savitri's real beginning happened not in her youth, but at the time society told her she had nothing left to offer. When her son left her behind, she could have withered. But she didn't. She paused. Then she planted.

She planted hope.

In the form of letters tucked under pillows, tea shared with Ammaji, paintings on cold, gray walls. She offered not miracles, but moments. Small, deliberate, beautiful moments that changed everything around her.

Ashray Nivas bloomed because one woman decided that sorrow did not have to be the end.

And that is what When the Sun Rose Again is truly about. It's about the kind of beginning that happens deep inside you, the one no one sees until suddenly, you're singing again.

We often think beginnings must follow youth. But what of the rest of us? What about the old man who once wrote poetry but hasn't picked up a pen in thirty years? What about the woman who still dreams of dancing but lives in a body that doesn't move as it used to? What about those who feel discarded, invisible?

This book reminds us that beginnings are not reserved for the young or the celebrated.

Beginnings can arrive in wheelchairs. In walkers. In quiet smiles.

They arrive when someone says, "Sing for me." Or "Tell me your story." Or simply, "You matter."

At Ashray Nivas, new beginnings looked like:

A music circle under a banyan tree.

A wall turned into a mural of memories.

A birthday celebration for a nurse who'd forgotten she mattered.

A spring mela with the scent of pickles and the sound of shayaris.

An old woman, once forgotten, becoming the heartbeat of a forgotten place.

Beginnings are not always loud. They do not always arrive with certainty. But they are there, waiting. All it takes is a light. A spark. A single act of love to begin again.

And Savitri did that, not once, but every day she chose to give when she herself had been denied.

What Will You Begin?

Now that this story has ended, ask yourself, what will you begin?

Will you call someone you've forgotten? Will you write to someone who believed you never would? Will you visit a place where people wait not for death, but for dignity?

Let this book not just be something you read. Let it be a mirror. Let it be a seed.

Because every time you:

Forgive someone.

Listen without interrupting.

Choose love over silence.

See worth in someone the world has left behind...

...you are planting a beginning.

Let Ashray Nivas live on, not just in fiction, but in real homes, real cities, real hearts.

Savitri's book, her last gift to the world, is not just a tribute to her life. It is an invitation.

We often look for magic in big moments. But this story tells us that the real kind of magic, the kind that heals, transforms, and connects, lives in the tiniest acts.

A letter slipped into a drawer. A photograph placed beside a hospital bed. A song hummed by a tired voice.

These are the ways we begin again.

When the sun rose again, it rose not because something changed outside, but because something changed within. Inside Savitri. Inside Ammaji. Inside Dinesh Uncle. Inside every resident who dared to feel again.

And now, perhaps, inside you.

So, let the sun rise again. Let it rise in your arms when you hug someone who thought they were forgotten. Let it rise in your voice when you read this story aloud to someone who needs to believe in hope. Let it rise in your tears, yes, but also in your actions.

Because Savitri didn't die a legend. She died a woman who lived.

And in doing so, she gave us all something eternal:

The truth that new beginnings don't need time. They just need courage.

And now, with this book in your hands, that courage belongs to you.

Let the sun rise again. And again. And again.

Public's Reflections On Grandparents

The little red chair sitting in my home for the past 12 years always reminds me of the true and unconditional love I received from my grandfather. I still remember the day a friend from the neighborhood didn't let me sit on his little chair, and that very evening, my Nanaji brought home a cute red chair just for me.

My mother often clears out old items and sells scrap, but this chair, though worn out and broken, is something I simply cannot let go of. It holds too many memories and too much love.

Grandparents are truly special. Their love is something you often realize the value of only after they're gone. Now, at 17, I miss my grandfather deeply, the way he carried me on his shoulders, how I would lie on his chest and fall asleep for hours. The day I lost him, I felt like I had lost half my world.

But God, in His kindness, left behind a blessing, my beautiful, simple, and elegant grandmother, my Nani. She wrapped us in her love, gave us strength, and never let us feel the absence of our grandfather. She was our rock.

But perhaps heaven was in need of good souls, and so He called her too, too soon for us, but just in time for Him.

- Aarush Manyala, 17 years old.

Grandparents are more different and older versions of your parents. Personally, they are more not used to the morden generation or even understand it. But no matter what, they were and will be the most kindest and one of the most trusted people you could have.

- Aarish Raj Saxena, 13 years old.

There are people who walk into our lives and quietly build the very foundation of who we are. For me and my brother, that foundation was our grandparents. They weren't just elders who watched us grow, they were the gentle teachers of our childhood, the soft cushions to fall back on, and the strongest pillars holding our little world together. Today, they are no longer with us, and yet, somehow, they are everywhere.

Our grandparents taught us everything, not through long lectures or textbooks, but in the quiet, everyday moments. They showed us the value of honesty when they kept their promises even when it was inconvenient. They taught us humility not by preaching it, but by living simply and giving generously. They taught us how to learn, not just in classrooms, but from people, nature, mistakes, and even heartbreak. And most importantly, they gave us permission to fall, to stumble, to cry, to be human, because they always believed we had it in us to rise again.

They loved us in a way that didn't demand anything in return. Their love was warm tea on cold evenings, soft lullabies during afternoon naps, wrinkled hands that held ours through every storm. In their eyes, we saw our best selves, even when we were flawed, even when we felt like we weren't enough. They had a way of making us feel safe in a world that often felt too loud, too fast, too much.

Now that they're gone, the silence they've left behind is deafening. Birthdays feel emptier, festivals a little duller. It's in the little things, the empty chair at the dinner table, the missing phone call after a long day, the quiet house that once echoed with laughter. You begin to understand the true weight of absence when the ones who shaped your soul are no longer around to hold it.

We used to think grandparents were forever. In many ways, they still are. Their stories, their values, their voices, they live on in us. In how we speak, in how we treat others, in the way we laugh or hold a cup of tea, we are their legacy. But no matter how much time passes, the ache remains. Some losses don't heal; they shape.

To anyone who still has their grandparents, hug them tighter, listen longer, and never take their presence for granted. Because one day, you'll search for them in the sky, in dreams, in old photographs and fading memories, and you'll wish for just one more moment, one more story, one more touch.

This reflection is for our beloved grandparents, for being our first teachers, our quiet protectors, and the love we will carry for the rest of our lives. You may no longer walk beside us, but you live in every step we take.

We miss you. We remember you. We will always love you.

-Ananya Anand, 19 years old.

I didn't get to spend much time with my grandparents, but the few memories I have are treasures I hold close to my heart. I can still recall how my dadi would lovingly call out to me for tea, gently settling me beside her as she fed me sips with her own hands, her eyes full of warmth, her touch so comforting. Though she left us when I was just two, that small act of love has stayed with me, quietly shaping my understanding of care. My dadaji was my safe place, I remember curling up next to him at night, asking him to tell me stories about our family. His voice, steady and soft, carried the weight of generations, and in those quiet moments, I felt the kind of love that doesn't fade, even with time.

- Aarav Anand, 13 years old.

My grandmother's stories were a source of comfort and wonder, each tale wrapping me in a world of imagination and warmth that still influences the way I see life today. One of my most cherished memories with my grandfather happened when I visited him in Bhopal unexpectedly. At first, he didn't recognize me, but as soon as our eyes met, his face softened, and he wrapped me in a tight, loving hug. After my father passed away, some Ashram visitors came to suggest my mother join them. I stood by her, gently turning them away, and in that quiet moment, my grandfather, who had listened intently, turned to me and said, "I hope you will handle the family and take care of your mother." His words, simple yet full of love, left a deep impression on my heart, reminding me of the responsibility and trust that ran through the generations.

    - **Priyanka Singh Bhadouriya, 33 years old.**

Questions You Might Ask

What moment in Savitri's story moved you the most?

How do you think society can change to embrace the elderly better?

Do you believe Arjun's love was enough, despite his choices? Why or why not?

Which secondary character did you connect with, and why?

If you had to write a letter to someone from your past, who would it be?

Final Words

Savitri didn't rise again as a phoenix in a grand, magical moment.

She did not roar back into youth, nor was she carried off by a thunderous miracle. No. She rose softly, like dew evaporating into morning light, like a melody hummed in an empty corridor, like the delicate rustle of paper as her final words took shape under a trembling hand.

She rose quietly, through song, songs hummed during sleepless nights and laughter-filled evenings; through kindness, offered without condition, without applause; through bangles gifted to trembling wrists, and shawls draped over frail shoulders with love that needed no words.

She rose through letters slipped under doors, unsigned but unforgettable. Through stories shared beneath flickering lights, as the past was given new breath and old hearts found rhythm again. Through eyes that once stared blankly into time, now gleaming with remembrance.

Her life did not end in silence. It ended in fullness. Not with grand farewells, but with the whispered thank yous of those she had healed. Not with sorrow, but with the quiet contentment of someone who had finally arrived, not at a destination, but at peace.

When the Sun Rose Again, it wasn't just the dawn peeking past the dusty windows of Ashray Nivas. It wasn't just the light creeping onto the checkered floors or warming the benches in the garden.

It was something far deeper.

It was the rising of hope in tired hearts, the kind of hope that does not shout, but stays.

It was the rising of memory in forgotten minds, like the first flower blooming after a drought.

It was the rising of forgiveness in long-held regrets, as sons and daughters whispered apologies that never made it in time.

It was the rising of community, of togetherness, in a place once known only for separation.

It was the rising of love, in corners where it had long been absent, in hearts where it had been left to sleep.

Ashray Nivas was no longer a place of endings. It had become a place of new beginnings. A sanctuary not of abandonment, but of rebirth.

And now, dear reader, that sun, that very sun, rises in your hands.

Every time you choose presence over forgetting.
Every time you listen when it's easier to ignore.
Every time you sit with someone, not out of duty, but out of love.
Every time you forgive.
Every time you remember.
Every time you choose love over silence.

The sun does not rise for the powerful alone. It rises for those who wait. For those who endure. For those who love, even when no one is watching.

Let it rise in your home.
Let it rise in your heart.
Let it rise in your words.
Let it rise when you touch the hands that time has wrinkled.
Let it rise when you sit beside someone whose story is nearly done.
Let it rise when you begin to write your own.

Let it rise again.
And again.
And again.

Until we all become the sunrise for someone else.

Until we all remember that when the sun rose again, it rose within us.

We often remember too late.

We wait until the chairs are empty and the voices have faded into memory before we realize who really mattered. We promise ourselves we'll visit next weekend, call tomorrow, write someday. And someday becomes never. We convince ourselves that our lives are too full, too busy to slow down for those who once carried us, fed us, sang to us, waited up for us.

But this book is not just Savitri's story. It is the story of every forgotten parent, every silenced grandparent, every elder whose name has become a whisper in their own home.

It is a quiet reminder that regret does not come like thunder, it comes softly, when it is already too late.

If you are reading this and someone you love is still alive, call them.

If they are near, hold their hand.

If they are far, write to them, not when you find time, but now.

Because memories don't ask for grand gestures. They ask for presence. They ask for love in its simplest form, time, kindness, acknowledgement.

No parent should feel like a burden. No grandparent should sit by the window, waiting for a voice that never comes.

We owe them more.

Not out of guilt.

But out of love.

This story is my way of saying what so many never get the chance to say:

"I'm sorry I didn't see you sooner. I'm sorry I forgot you were once the sun in my sky."

Let us not wait for ashes and eulogies to speak our love.

Let us live it, now.

For when we choose remembrance over regret, when we choose to sit beside the aged rather than look away, when we choose them, we are choosing the best parts of ourselves.

And then, truly...

When the sun rises again, it will rise through us.